T0151297

INCIDENT LIGHT

Also by H. L. Hix

POETRY
Legible Heavens *
God Bless *
Chromatic *
Shadows of Houses *
Surely As Birds Fly
Rational Numbers
Perfect Hell

ARTISTS' BOOKS AND LIMITED EDITIONS
This Translucent Tissue (artist's book by Judi Ross)
The Last Hour (artist's book by Egidijus Rudinskas)
Intellectual Pleasures (limited edition by Aralia Press)

TRANSLATIONS
Jüri Talvet, *Estonian Elegy: Selected Poems*, trans. with the author
Juhan Liiv, *The Mind Would Bear No Better*, trans. with Jüri Talvet
On the Way Home: An Anthology of Contemporary Estonian Poetry,
trans. with Jüri Talvet
Jüri Talvet, *A Call for Cultural Symbiosis*, trans. with the author
Eugenijus Ališanka, *City of Ash*, trans. with the author

THEORY AND CRITICISM
Wild and Whirling Words: A Poetic Conversation *
As Easy As Lying: Essays on Poetry *
Understanding William H. Gass
Understanding W. S. Merwin
Spirits Hovering Over the Ashes: Legacies of Postmodern Theory
Morte d'Author: An Autopsy

* Also published by Etruscan Press

INCIDENT LIGHT

Poems by

H. L. Hix

etruscan press

Etruscan Press
Wilkes University
84 West South Street
Wilkes-Barre, PA 18766

 WILKES UNIVERSITY

www.etruscanpress.org

Printed in the United States of America

Publisher's Cataloging-in-Publication
(Provided by Quality Books, Inc.)

    Hix, H. L.
       Incident light / H.L. Hix. -- 1st ed.
       p. cm.
       Poems.
       ISBN-13. 978-0-9745995-1-9
       ISBN-10: 0-9745995-1-4

       I. Title.

    PS3558.I88I53 2009   811'.54
                      QBI09-600161

First Edition

Design by Michael Ress

Etruscan Press is committed to sustainability and environmental stewardship. We elected to print this title through Bookmobile on FSC paper that contains 30% post consumer fiber manufactured using biogas energy and 100% wind power.

About This Book

When my friend the artist Petra Soesemann learned at forty-nine that the dad who had raised her from birth was not her biological father, her life seemed to me instantly mythical. Wanting to write into that life, I thought first to do so as fiction (any resemblance to persons living or dead...), but on second thought sought biography. Of a sort: biography whose first fidelity is not to facts, but to imagination, biography that *loosens* reality's hold, releases the life into lyric. Nothing attested, everything sung.

The epigraph comes from C. L. Hardin's *Color for Philosophers*. To it might have been added the question Miranda poses Prospero in *The Tempest*: "Are you not my father?" The poem "Your mother must have been very attractive" re-presents information from Semir Zeki's *Inner Vision*.

My thanks to the editors who granted prior publication to certain of these poems.

Alabama Literary Review	"Do you believe in ghosts?"
	"How would you change your life if you could?"
Clackamas Literary Review	"Did others know?"
Colorado Review	"What is your favorite song?"
	"When did you first learn about your father?"
	"What have you kept secret for years?"
	(He alone...)
The Iowa Review	"I see now where your features come from."
	(Dad loved cars...)
Margie	"How old was your Dad when he died?"
Poetry	"*Night Watch*"
	"*Beyond (A System for Passing)*"
A Public Space	"Did you ever suspect anything...?"
Salt Hill	"How do you feel about having new sisters?"
	(We'd have been...)
	"Where does your name come from?"
	(Sometimes I mail...)
Washington Square	"*The Dresden Codex*"
Whiskey Island	"*Shawabty Box of Ditamenpaankh*"
	"*Feathered Panel*"

I am grateful to Sharon Dynak and the Ucross Foundation for a residency that helped me turn research and reflection into a draft, and of course most of all to Petra herself for suffering hours and hours of interviews, for giving me access to personal journals, papers, and other materials, and for permission to tell her story in this way.

Table of Contents

An object turns out to have a transmission color, a reflection color, an interference color, etc., no two necessarily the same, and each color is a function of detection angle as well as of the spectrum of the incident light.

Where did you grow up?

Long years back they took out the tracks on that stretch
that cleft the town clean in two. Take-backs taken,
that stagnant place stayed strapped instead of staunching
the spill of sons and daughters to Columbus
and Cleveland. No trains track that parallel now,
but then they punctured my fear-perforated,
fit-stippled sleep. My whole girlhood, not one night
passed but a train-horn's warning winced me awake.

Did you ever suspect anything when you were growing up?

It just started one day, that eerie screaming,
my inconsolability given voice,
given back as if from some bird or from trees.
The new couple's child down the street simply screamed,
a train whistle no longer pretending grief,
its long wail every little while a perfect
loneliness; an owl lifting its prey, every
little while, hour into hour, night after day.

What is your favorite song?

In Peru, defining the descent toward
el pueblo Paracas and the Pacific,
a small oasis they call Huacachina
asserts itself to spite the surrounding sand.
Since the sea wants to be mountains, and mountains
to be sea, the coast, imprisoned between one
vain desire and its equal opposite, drones
desert dunes that mimic wave and peak alike.

You must have loved your dad.

He'd worn it out, the ragged cotton dress shirt
he gave me to paint in in kindergarten,
English all day in school but German at home.
I wanted to sleep in that shirt, to wear it
always, I cried when they made me take it off.
I tried to talk, but knew only how to paint
and cry. To this day a man in a white shirt
makes me speak in primary colors and tears.

Where does your name come from?

Sometimes I mail them to made-up addresses,
these letters I've started writing him, to share
secrets I kept from him while he was alive,
to ask him all I wish I'd known but did not.
Sometimes I mail them to myself, posting them
from places he never saw, throwing them out
when I return, because we need from them not
my words given him but his voice given back.

Shawabty Box of Ditamenpaankh

Whether to plow the fields or fill the channels
with water or carry sand from East to West,
so charge I these shawabtys on our behalf,
for you who have made pilgrimage already
to Abydos, and for me, who'll follow soon.
Give over labor; these spirits precede me.
Though they merely mimic with blue the faience
who could afford, they bring tools, and know their charge.

How do you feel about having new sisters?

We'd have been fifteen then, Roxanne and I, that
middle of the night, when we snuck out of her
father's house, who knows how come, and walked a block
to the used-car lot and sat, why not, in one
at a time — it was a different time, a small
town, they all were unlocked with the key inside —
and smoked and listened to the radio. We
were fifteen that small-town sneak-out-and-smoke night.

I see now where your features come from.

Dad loved cars, would have studied engineering,
but they could send only one son to school, so
he stayed, worked in the family bakery.
That's why they look so happy to me here: his
fedora tilted toward the black sedan,
the buttons on their coats echoing headlights
and hubcaps, arm in arm, her calves and ankles
bare, her weight on one foot, the other tiptoe.

Do your half-sisters consider themselves German or Turkish?

Everyone smoked back then. Three of us, women,
closet office, two at a time, they took turns,
my bosses, one there the other in New York
for two weeks, then switch. Back then I didn't *ask*
my life to make sense. They were lovers. At nine
I arrived, opened the door, smoke poured out, there
sat one boss smoking, arguing on the phone
with the other. Why *should* it make sense? Sobbing.

Der Struwwelpeter

This I knew before I knew anything else:
I needed some richer way to see, beyond
the girl with ribboned braids who'd played with matches
and now teetered on one foot, arms raised before
a cape of flame and clouds of smoke, then (next frame)
her empty shoes, and two cats wiping their eyes
over the smoldering ash that had been her,
each wearing one of her ribbons on its tail.

What have *you* kept secret for years?

She matched her hands flat to the jambs just like this,
blocking the office doorway, light behind her
from the library windows. She looked dirty,
like someone stoking a boiler. I *saw* it,
the dark field around her, dinge-smoke and coal dust.
She'd bought a gun, but who knew till she used it.
Some people level out in time, others not.
Light behind her, she the delta for its silt.

What were you most afraid of as a child?

Finding myself at night with two drunk murderers
riding in a rusted-out Ford stationwagon
        begs some explanation.
        Start with Cleveland winters.
That year's had borne down hard, seemed even more severe
than normal for that gray place, longer and colder
than any past winter anyone there would bear
        to name or remember.
This was six or eight years after everyone else
had hitchhiked out to California, but a friend
(now a journalist in Jordan and Lebanon)
had a place close to the bay in San Francisco,
all the excuse another friend and I needed
        to decide we would go.
We hadn't given consequences too much thought
        or planned the whole thing out.
I must have thought the weather would warm steadily
the farther one went west of Cleveland, the nearer
one drew to ever-sunny California, so
        a jacket's all I wore.
We got rides pretty quickly, mostly with truckers,
        all of them real talkers.
In Iowa, though, not halfway across, we hit
a storm, a major blizzard with snowflakes I swear

as big as my hand, so they closed the highway down
and our truck had to leave the road at the next stop,

     with three hundred others.

     They ran out of food soon.

     We sat, 48 hours.

We scavenged our backpacks — bags of carrots, fig bars —

     and shared with the truckers.

Others must learn sooner what I only gathered
then, that a life might never make sense: there I sat,
trying to make myself into a person,
at a place that was a place only because one
highway crossed another there, in a window booth
butt-to-butt with some trucker twice my age, staring
through a blizzard over fuel pumps at a porn store,
thinking if I want fries and a burger well-done
I'm shit out of luck, but if I want a dildo,

     I can have a dozen.

Once they cleared the highway, we headed west again,
but I'd been disillusioned: even the mountains

     now seemed god-forsaken.

We'd crossed into California before the last
rig left us at a truck stop, we assumed stranded
for the night, until a couple overheard us
worrying, said they'd take us to San Francisco,

that's where they were headed.
Seems dumb now, but we'd been on the road long enough
that even that ragged pair with their ramshackle
wagon looked better than refills of thin coffee
and staring down at a formica tabletop,
so instead of waiting there five hours for daybreak,
            my friend put down his cup.
            I picked up my backpack.

That's how we got in the car; what we needed then
            was to get out again.
We hadn't picked up on how drunk — or high — they were
            till we were in the car.
I wouldn't have had to do it, she protested
(as if I had accused her) over and over,
the whiskey strong on her breath, *if she hadn't been*
            movin' in on my man.
            The "she" was her best friend.
            The "it" was stabbing her.
            In Vegas, in a bar.
Bitch was my best friend from when we were kids, third grade,
we started smoking the same day from the same pack,
lost our virginity (her uncle doesn't count,
though maybe that made her less afraid than me)

the same car the same night (she was in the back seat,
I was in the front, the boys were cousins, we knew
mine from school, hers was in from outta town, shoulda
seen my boy, he was beautiful, had dark eyes, hair
to make a crow look pale, tattoo on his shoulder,
and everything below in good working order,
plus he was four years older, could drive, had a car),
still it's just a rule: never ever let no one
have a piece of your man, even a little bit,

        cause she sure will want more.

She had red hair and freckles, her nose slanted
toward the left corner of her mouth, her nails
were bitten to the quick, she kept leaning closer
and closer, her face next to mine, the whiskey smell
overwhelming, same story, same stabbing, same friend,

        told over and over.

        The man was no better.

She'd chosen Canada to flee toward instead
of Mexico, met him — blind luck — in Montana,
the parking lot of the motel they'd both chosen,
the day he'd been released from max, double murder
(*about the time I was born*, she laughed) but early

        out for good behavior.

They were just driving, no destination, waiting

for the law to forget them, carrying all their
not-much in the back of the wagon, a big pile
of her clothes, a small pile of his, a cardboard box
        of pans and silverware.
My friend was smart enough to plead too much coffee,
request a bathroom break, and then suggest they must
be tired from being on the road, all that driving,
        why not let one of us.
So he drove the rest of the way, one murderer
asleep against the passenger door, the other
        leaning on my shoulder.
Our lie that when light broke they'd see the Pacific
from that very parking lot where we were idling
bought us time: soon they were sleeping and we were free
to find a pay phone, call our friend for directions
now we'd arrived, uncertain how to be happy
just to be alive when all we really felt was
        tired and cold and hungry.

What are you most afraid of now?

Flu's high fever had me near delirium.
Front door open, the heat, screened-in porch door latched.
He had a wrench and a shaggy dog story,
gotta help my father fix his broke-down truck,
stuck in Lawrence, five bucks for gas, pay you back.
Swinging a wrench the whole time, swinging a wrench.
Hot that day. My wallet, a five and some ones.
More embellishments, even after the bills.

Where did you grow up?

Without regard. Might as well have been those words,
the horn's forlorn keening at 4:22
every morning, then again at 12:19
and 5:37 of an afternoon.
*That one drought summer, sure the damn'd rain 'd come
of an afternoon*, that's how I learned the phrase,
*but wouldn' no more 'n rearrange the dust
to little stars on them brittle brown corn leaves.*

Did you ever suspect anything when you were growing up?

In my mind the screaming child was a boy, though
on no evidence I could name. Even on
a walk, strapped into that oversized stroller,
he screamed. Who knew what was wrong. No neighbors spoke
to the family, who soon moved. No one asked.
How could they, and say they kept to themselves? Scared
first, I guess, then embarrassed, but soon enough
they could complain again about the starlings.

What did you *feel* when you first found out?

That first one, a cotton button-up, paisley
patterned, not flattering, my hair was short then,
I was young, they all said it made me look like
a boy, but I stained it down to elbow fray
and followed it with shirt after shirt, thrift-store
finds or gifts from friends, lucky shirts that soon had
to be pink so when my car broke down someone
would help. When one wore out I found another.

How do you feel about having new sisters?

It was a different time, it was a small town,
so when I lied, *I'm looking for my lost dog,*
Officer Hale knew what to hear: *I'm fifteen,*
it's the middle of the night, I want to smoke
and listen to the radio with my friend.
He knew to say *Go home* — it was a small town.
Go home, look for your dog tomorrow. He knew
Roxanne was hiding. He knew where not to look.

Night Watch

As gestures to beckon geometry's end
I post letters to my lost Mayan sisters,
solicit layers sussed from layers to test
history, push past parallel. Mystery
becomes you, Mother, as does the lust the rest
of us suffer, lust you must once have induced.
What perceptions I trust defy perspective.
I take my troubles scribbled, not erased.

What have *you* kept secret for years?

He alone in darkness when all else was light.
Without believing in pearls, he'd ridden stones
down to a depth he knew his lungs might not match.
Twice that long month of leave-taking I saw him,
and seeing him I saw, too, the murk, saw him
swim through thick darkness while we others breathed light.
The turbidity that submerged him, I saw
as real. I *saw* it. As real as this table.

Why the fascination with candles?

My uncle's answering the phone surprised me;
maybe he was working on my parents' place.
Camping? What do you mean you're going camping?
Just for two days, this great place in Wisconsin.
Why had I called at all? I never phoned in
with my weekend plans. He must have thought I knew.
You can't go camping. Didn't your Mom tell you?
No, though by then I'd begun to understand.

When did you first learn about your father?

Snow, plenty deep already, coming down fast.
I couldn't *talk* with that old man, the tv
news was on, he kept complaining niggers this
and niggers that. The hotel owner wouldn't
take my check, but the old man would. *I'm retired* —
breath in gasps — *I need the money.* Had to wheel
this oxygen tank behind him when he walked.
The blizzard wouldn't let up. We watched the news.

After the Sumerian

Have you seen how things stand? Must what must be be?
If I creaked secrets, my daughter, dreamed to you
the rust taste, spore smell, rustled movement through that
moonlessness, you would buckle as before you
I bent. Hands that held yours, arms that embraced you
crumble, lice-laced, worm-warmed. None returns. Cracks gasp
parched ground's thirst but fill with dust. So spoken to,
the daughter clutched her knees, wept herself to sleep.

What is your favorite song?

The pueblo was pale, monotone, sand-colored.
Even the tiny lake — this was a desert —
and the sunbeaten boardwalk that bounded it
looked bleached-out. Noon, no shade to slake the thin hue
all things thirsted to. Across the lake, though, eight
squat adobe changing booths sheltered shadows.
Looters, wind, and sun had stolen their curtains.
Perfectly even, that row, holes in a flute.

How would you change your life if you could?

As a kid my favorite food was shrimp.
Must have rubbed pencil lead in your eyes.
I liked what my dad liked; he liked shrimp.
The welts on my belly looked like eyes.

Must've rubbed pencil lead in your eyes.
Alcohol for turning twenty-one.
The welts on my belly looked like eyes.
She listed my symptoms to the phone.

Alcohol helped turn me twenty-one.
Thank god someone had stayed in the room.
So many symptoms into the phone.
Get her to the emergency room.

Thank god someone else was in the room.
Anaphylactic shock swells your throat.
Get her to the emergency room!
Sooner or later you suffocate.

Anaphylactic shock swelled my throat,
my lips went numb, I flowered with welts.
Sooner or later you suffocate.
They make interns work those weekend shifts.

My lips went numb. My skin bloomed with welts.
Sounds like allergies, take off your shirt.
Interns pinballed through those weekend shifts,
fistfight- and car-wreck-filled Friday nights.

Sounds like allergies, take off your shirt.
Shrimp, bloody mary, then lobster, beer.
Bar brawls and car wrecks for Friday night.
I thought first I could just take a shower.

Shrimp, bloody mary, lobster, and beer.
As a kid my favorite food was shrimp.
I thought if I could just take a shower.
What my dad liked, I liked; he liked shrimp.

What are you most afraid of now?

Come next day, police came, gave a description
of the same man, had I seen him yesterday?
Yeah, sure. His story'd made no sense, but whose
does, I gave him a few bucks, he went away.
He wasn't fixing a truck with just that wrench,
but I was sick, I couldn't think. *Ma'am, the man
around the corner, just three houses down, is in
intensive care.* My door'd been open, the heat.

Where did you grow up?

Back when it still shook black trestles, back when words
were ladling me language to language, the train
changed schedule for no one and nothing, not for
the neighbor's sleeping in after always one
too many the night before, not for how long
at this latitude the reluctant sun takes
to rise over all that snowmelt mud, not for
no rusted-out Rambler caught at the crossing.

Did you ever suspect anything when you were growing up?

I recall nothing of her features, just that
same scarf each day, pastel blue. Her child's scream, though,
that, my first mosaic visit to the vast
land past pain, past specific grief, I relive.
The scream repeated something he alone heard,
as bats hear inhuman frequencies and steer
by them, as a mystic hears spirits and prays,
asking nothing, willfully forfeiting will.

Do your half-sisters consider themselves German or Turkish?

I was thin myself from my year in Peru,
but hadn't known her at first when I got back.
Oh, you wouldn't recognize her now, she's lost
electrolytes, that's what anorexia
does, that and make your hair go brittle, take back
a lot of weight, change even the way you look
at people. Never mind gaunt cheeks, bony hands.
The last time we talked, she seemed preoccupied.

From the German

Everything seems pregnant with its contrary.
Innocence is a splendid thing, only it
is always progressively becoming God.
The understanding is nothing to the heart
one must still have chaos in oneself to be.
People seldom die when you want to be sad.
Innocence is a splendid thing. Only it,
the understanding, is nothing to the heart.

Why the fascination with candles?

After a day or two they sent my dad home.
My grandmother lived with my parents by then,
and talked with him a lot those days — hours, really —
he was back. She said later he kept asking
about his father's death, how it had been, though
when I sat with him, he said hardly a word.
I'd never met my dad's father, knew nothing
of his death, know nothing of it to this day.

When did you first learn about your father?

He laid out a pair of his own pyjamas
for me, that old man did. Most of the hotel
had been converted to dark, cramped apartments.
He fixed me a tv dinner, the old kind,
foil-covered. Made me sleep in his bed, new sheets,
he took the couch. Griped at all the tv news.
While the blizzard labored, burying my truck,
I slept under that bastard's oxygen tent.

How old was your dad when he died?

There they live still, my mother and grandmother,
in four wallpapered rooms above what had been
the bakery from which my father offered
one small town flavors from a bigger world than
it otherwise knew, before that bakery
became a travel agency for one year,
tattoo parlor for two more, and finally
the permanent backdrop of a For Lease sign.

Feathered Panel

Feathers from Peru's Papagayo macaw,
viewed from close enough and in good light, look green.
The blue feathers look green, so do the yellow.
As it was on that bird-riddled desert coast
a dozen centuries ago, so is it
here and now. We weave what we weave, blue feathers,
as offerings of what colors we can catch
to what colors — though we name them — we cannot.

What have *you* kept secret for years?

Gene Hearn: clean as you or me, but *looked* dirty.
Mother dead, he never said how, dad dead drunk.
Hardly talked, lived in what had been a boxcar.
Bathed, washed his own clothes. Still, that sooty shadow.
Ginger Kirsch, another classmate, same shadow.
I learned later that she'd learned sooner than us
and from her father what should be learned later,
from others, and what no one should have to learn.

I see now where your features come from.

My father, years before he was my father,
wearing white to isolate his face — my face —
from all those *patterns*: carpets, wallpaper, lace,
his mother's busy dress, the chairs' upholstery.
My father, his parents, and framed within this
photo of a family of whom I know
little, another photo of another
family, of whom I know nothing at all.

What is your favorite song?

I followed the lake back to where a cluster
of dusty, thirsty trees clung to a tiny
adobe house. I was just walking, taking
everything in, trying to earn the trust of
such reticent starkness. I stopped, stood, stared hard
at the freckled patch of shade cooling a pale
adobe house that had been overgrown by —
now stood submerged beneath — a bougainvillea.

Do you believe in ghosts?

He knows your name? You told him where you live and where you work?
        A stranger confesses double murder,
lays out plans to kill his own wife, and you give him your card?
        I could tell friends what happened, but not why.
I'd spent a Fulbright year pursuing Peru, wooing it,
        learning how little I'd known about light,
believing weaving outstays stone, keeps more constant color,
        thinking this place might make mortals mistake
themselves for gods, twenty thousand feet from snow to the sea.

I couldn't get my suitcase open. I'd sent some things on,
        but this was a time of terrorists there,
the guards inspected everything, matched passenger to bag,
        let nothing undefended on the plane.
When they asked how much I'd spent in my stay, I caused delay
        by telling the truth (a mistake), and had
to explain I'd spent six hundred, yes, but been there a year.
        So I'd been a long time in this office
before we got to the bag I'd had to sit on to close,
        and now couldn't open, nor could the guard.
Even after a year there I was naïve, kept trying
        to open the suitcase so long they had
to hold the plane for me before — at last — I realized

that all it took for the guard to see things
my way was a bottle of pisco from my carry-on.

They had to open the door again to let me on board.
        They seated me beside an older man
(I was young then, all men were older) and we didn't speak.
        The flight from Lima was how long? nine hours?
with a layover in Panama. I was tired. I slept.
        At some point they handed out the customs
declaration form that asks how much you're bringing back.
        I had seven thousand dollars on me,
all the savings of the woman from whom I had rented
        my last months in Peru, trusted to me
on my promise to send her daughter in the states a check.
        Not having asked then why the cash couldn't
go through a bank, I couldn't construct now a good guess what
        to declare, and the man beside me saw
my hesitation. *Just declare a souvenir or two.*
        If it had grounding, it wouldn't be trust.
I didn't say how much I had, but did ask him, *This line*
        for cash, what's the best way to fill it out?
He showed me his form that said $25, then smiled
        and opened his vest: wads and wads of bills,
like in the movies, with bands around them. *Don't sweat*, he said.

I'm a businessman, I carry twenty
or thirty thousand to Chicago all the time. No one
        will ask. That started the conversation,
some Spanish, more English, even a little in German.

He hadn't learned how quick he was with languages until
        the war — they had taught nothing so fancy
in school where he grew up, and then he was motivated,
        it made him useful to the officers,
earned him details as safe as anything there at the front.
        It helps now in business, he said, but then
it meant much more: a little distance from the line of fire.
        North Pole, Siberia, Antarctica,
no place gets colder than Germany in January,
        has wind so penetrating, snow so deep.
By then he'd forgotten me, focused his eyes somewhere else.
        They were our allies — "they" were the Russians —
but rations were scarce, and their icons didn't make them saints,
        read how many German women they raped
when they took Berlin. He and a buddy were transporting
        two Russians on foot, he didn't say why.
Reunite them with their unit, maybe. Wasn't the point.
        He and his buddy were scared and hungry,

afraid of frostbite, of getting lost, running out of food.

    They decided to kill the two Russians.

It might have been exactly what they were supposed to do,

    just orders that can't be given out loud.

By this time his chin was quivering, and tears streaked both cheeks.

    The look on their faces. They'd trusted us.

All these years, I've tried to justify it, tried to forget.

But misery follows misery, and guilt follows guilt,

    so he wasn't through. He had bodyguards

in Peru, everyone with money did, kidnapping had

    become a common crime, though bodyguards

didn't always stop it, they could be corrupted, become

    the kidnappers. He had a family

in Chicago, a daughter he loved, a wife he didn't.

    He was in love now with someone younger.

Divorce would give his wife sole custody of their daughter.

    His wife came with him to Peru sometimes,

he could have his bodyguards hand her off to someone else

    to do her in. He had it all worked out.

Still teary-eyed, mind you, which is why my friends were worried.

    All I could think to say was, *Anything*

that began that way couldn't end well, that's not how you want

to start a life with the woman you love.
He thought for a while, a long while, said *You're probably right.*

The layover in Panama ended his reverie.
Back on the plane, I showed him the molas
I'd bought, listened to him dismiss folk art, then tell about
his collection, prints and master drawings.
That's it. No other dangerous intimacies, shocking
disclosures. The import/export business
is dull, really. No later threat confirmed my friends' concerns.
He must be dead by now. He trusted me
with his story. He gave me his card, so I gave him mine.

Where did you grow up?

Without regard, giving us no good goddamn,
that damned horn again, then for four long minutes
chunk-chunka-chunk from a few hundred axles
in perpetual contest to count the joints
where rail reasons not quite seamlessly to rail,
loud in the summer through pried-open windows,
louder after snow shushed all else to softness,
loudest when starlight insisted all be still.

Did you ever suspect anything when you were growing up?

Less an alien threat than the self my self
that gone small-town summer gave over for good
to perdition not punishment but mere fact,
his scream, slipping across my bedroom sill or
creeping up behind me in the yard back when
"disturbed" seemed description enough, now blossoms
the dissonant orange of poppies, the name
and color of what is much too much to bear.

From the German

What is real is experienced in impulse.
We meant something other than we meant to mean.
Suffering is a condition of all truth
and everything happens as it does happen.
Spirits reveal themselves only to spirits,
draw to themselves all the creatures of the air.
We meant something other than we meant to mean,
and everything happens as it does happen.

Why the fascination with candles?

I think I should go back to the hospital.
He'd been home only a few days. It was five
in the morning, I'd been sleeping on the floor
in the living room, family had come in
even from Germany. He knew better than
to drive himself. *You don't mind driving me there?*
He whispered, woke only me. He didn't want
to upset my mother or disturb the guests.

When did you first learn about your father?

Sure, he'd get me going, the mechanic said,
but what was I doing driving in this snow?
Gotta get back to Chicago, work. *Hotel*
in town ain't much, but stop now. The old man who
saw me in the hotel lot, snow to my knees,
next morning called the Amish hardware store, this
was *early* but they came, warned me not to drive
in this stuff, filled my truck anyway with bricks.

When did you start smoking?

It had been fifty years since the "gentlemen's
conversation," twenty years since my dad died.
I think my father felt he'd held up his end
of their agreement to avoid all contact.
His letter was blunt, said he wanted closure.
When my mother had a small car accident,
she recognized that the few people alive
who could tell me were in her generation.

How old was your dad when he died?

She recognizes nothing, my grandmother,
of where she is now, or who my mother is,
though she does recall starving through the great war
on a tiny island below sea level
as all Holland is, and gives the memory
again and again in a dozen Dutch words
different from the other few Dutch words she wails
if Mother leaves her for even a moment.

Why did your mother tell you after all this time?

I'm floating in an inner tube when the tide
catches me and starts pulling me out to sea.
People on the beach start shouting. Dad is first
to swim out to save me, but doesn't make it,
drowns in the attempt. Mother leaves the beach then,
comes running back with my father, who pauses
to assess the situation. She's jumping
up and down, panicked. He swims out to save me.

What is your favorite song?

It buried me beneath some uncanny weight,
that can't-catch-my-breath I'm-being-watched feeling.
For one long moment it was speaking to me,
a bougainvillea, a magenta color
mere suggestion of which to this day evokes
that flower's voice, murmurs a mode of knowing
that has roots, gives me for one moment a way
of reasoning with unreasonable light.

The Dresden Codex

To compensate for another offering,
the codex Cortés confiscated from your
shrine centuries ago, I give *this*, Ix Chel,
all of it, as prayer for my Mayan sisters,
be they where they may. May their births be given
them again, as mine was given back to me.
May this prayer, like that first offering,
be born from what fires find it, what floods follow.

What was that book you were reading?

Sulfur shelf fungus: best meal I ever had.
A friend back from deep-sea fishing with his dad
seared me some tuna he'd caught, a huge fillet,
with this ugly yellow fungus, hideous,
off a dead log in his back yard. *Been waiting,*
he said, *to harvest it.* My disbelief bled.
Just wait. Cut in cubes, sauteed in olive oil.
Dead-dog ugly, but buttery, like lobster.

How did you learn English?

They brought ice down from the mountains. This was high
in the Andes, a pueblo with hot springs
but no electricity. I stayed because
the bus that brought me there came back when it could
or when the driver wanted, who knows. Propane,
no electricity, but ice from high up
and hot springs, tiny tiled bathrooms where you soak
a long time, no bus to catch, by candlelight.

Sex is turquoise.

It's not so hard to understand. Small town,
        post-war Germany,
beautiful young woman stands looking in a bookstore window,

        debonair, slightly older Turkish man,
                beautiful himself,
speaks to her. *Fräulein…* She corrects him: *Frau.* Nod of apology.

        She's walking, to escape even briefly
                the few narrow rooms
above her husband's father's bakery, where she lives with her

        quiet husband and his loud family.
                She's known her husband
since they were children, known always she would be married to him,

        passed up a scholarship to music school
                to stay at his side,
but not forgotten dreams of travel she knows she can't fulfill.

        So when they meet again at the market
                and he offers — *Frau*
this time — to carry her bags, she accepts with a flustered blush,

some part of her no less real than the rest
                given life again.
He's careful not to touch her, but would she do him the honor

        to meet him next afternoon for coffee,
                a conversation
on her way to or from some errand? He knows a shop nearby.

        Once for coffee turns into more than once,
                turns into long walks,
confidences. Her husband works odd hours, and the family —

        never time alone. This man meets her eyes,
                he *listens* to her.
After one walk, a chaste goodbye, his cheek barely touching hers.

        Another day, coffee and a long talk,
                he takes her fingers
lightly to help her from the chair, and she does not take them back.

Tell me a story about your mother.

There'd been a misunderstanding about dates.
He'd rent my place while I was in Mexico —
big house close to school, friend of a friend, why not? —
but he arrived an hour after I returned.
You shouldn't smoke. Where are the cereal bowls?
Then the war: I smoked and smoked, watching the news.
He ate my cereal from bowls I bought him.
We made friends — I loved him, I guess — but he's gone.

Do your half-sisters consider themselves German or Turkish?

It was rare for her, four days away from work.
They went to check, found her dead in a straight chair,
nearly upright, but with a different look.
Oh, you wouldn't recognize her now, she's lost
a lot of weight, she's got a different look.
She'd had a heart attack while painting her toes.
So absent, she looked like she'd been dead for months.
No, you wouldn't recognize her now, she's lost.

How old was your dad when he died?

That's not what I fear. What I fear is *living*,
turning into the old lady with the cats,
shuffling around her rundown house in slippers,
each day the same sad decades-out-of-date dress,
her skin sagging back to earth, fixed to her bones
at fewer and fewer points, mind dissolving
back to amniosis, fixed to fewer and
fewer moments, farther and farther away.

Why did your mother tell you after all this time?

If you were from around these parts, you'd know more
recipes for beef, you'd know not to ask me
how many cattle I own, you'd know we call
those crystals Pecos diamonds, you'd know you can
find as many as you like just by bending
down, pushing some dirt around, you'd know a draw
from a sinkhole, you'd know ways to find the spot
where it rained, and how to drive your cattle there.

Where did you grow up?

No traffic troubles the path that had been tracks
but the couple more or less my mother's age
who walk must-be-part-lab-because-what-mutt's-not
as early of a winter morning as light
allows, or in summer respect for neighbors' peace,
then again late of an afternoon, their lives
planed by the dog's insistences, sanded smooth
by winter light my mother's age, more or less.

SCOOTER! every few trestles, SCOO-OO-OO-TER!
trailed always by the same patter, word for word,
At's a good boy, you stick close now buddy,
we doan wancha gettin lost now do we? No,
what'd we do with all those table scraps? Mama
here'd give up her girlish figure if she
didn't feed you half her dinner every day,
long enough for Scooter to catch the next scent.

Bemusement must be enough for mama, who
lost her girlish figure three Scooters ago
to the bearing of Rusty Jr. or Meg
(who hasn't given them grandchildren, can't seem
to settle down or find someone, and seldom
visits). Bemusement must be just enough, that

and holding hands, twice a day the same straight route,
each time in no hurry, no hurry at all.

How did you learn English?

The mountainside itself made most of the wall —
they had to build around the springs — but the tubs
were tiled, and held two or three. The water steamed.
They used a metal rasp on chunks of ice brought
down from the mountain, shaved them into sno-cones
soaked in sweet yellow soda, Inca Cola.
No electricity. Sweat. That sweet shaved ice.
You soaked by candlelight, the rock walls steamed slick.

Your mother must have been very attractive.

Color results from the brain's comparison
of wavelength compositions: light reflected
off one surface with light from what surrounds it.
Color is the comparison, not the light,
a property of the brain, not of the world.
In the mountains, in winter, the sun rises
first in the snow: ghostly blue that defers to
its later, legitimate sister the sky.

When did you start smoking?

This one was taken not long after my birth.
I used to ask her why she'd dyed her hair dark.
She always replied, *That was the fashion then.*
The real reason is obvious to me now,
as it must have been then to everyone else
in that small town where before then she'd been blond.
I always envied my parents their blond hair
and blue eyes, having such dark features myself.

Did others know?

She sent him one baby picture, enclosed with
only the briefest note: *Her eyes speak of you.*
As she herself had never been able to.
He kept it those fifty years, he keeps it still,
in the family album — the note kept, too,
but hidden — deflecting others' inquiries.
Her eyes speak of you who must be otherwise
hidden, here in me, there *as* her, in plain view.

Beyond (A System for Passing)

To say how much I've missed you, I offer this,
at most mist, at least assorted letters, lists,
numbers I insist tell stories. I kissed you
last in the casket in which you passed beyond,
to some next place, but last listened for your voice
last night, these long years after, will listen next
when next oppressed by blue-gray, as I am now,
as I, thus lost, am always by your absence.

Books from Etruscan Press

Peal | Bruce Bond
The Disappearance of Seth | Kazim Ali
Toucans in the Arctic | Scott Coffel
Synergos | Roberto Manzano
Lies Will Take You Somewhere | Sheila Schwartz
Legible Heavens | H. L. Hix
A Poetics of Hiroshima | William Heyen
Saint Joe's Passion | J. D. Schraffenberger
American Fugue | Alexis Stamatis
Drift Ice | Jennifer Atkinson
The Widening | Carol Moldaw
Parallel Lives | Michael Lind
God Bless: A Political/Poetic Discourse | H. L. Hix
Chromatic | H. L. Hix (National Book Award finalist)
The Confessions of Doc Williams & Other Poems | William Heyen
Art into Life | Frederick R. Karl
Shadows of Houses | H. L. Hix
The White Horse: A Colombian Journey | Diane Thiel
Wild and Whirling Words: A Poetic Conversation | H. L. Hix
Shoah Train | William Heyen (National Book Award finalist)
Crow Man | Tom Bailey
As Easy As Lying: Essays on Poetry | H. L. Hix
Cinder | Bruce Bond
Free Concert: New and Selected Poems | Milton Kessler
September 11, 2001: American Writers Respond | William Heyen

Founded in 2001 with a generous grant from the Oristaglio Foundation, Etruscan Press is a non-profit cooperative of poets and writers working to produce and promote books that nurture the dialogue among genres, achieve a distinctive voice, and reshape the literary and cultural histories of which we are a part.

The Etruscan Press publication of the present edition of *Incident Light* has been made possible by a grant from the National Endowment for the Arts.

NATIONAL
ENDOWMENT
FOR THE ARTS
A great nation
deserves great art.

ETRUSCAN IS PROUD OF SUPPORT RECEIVED FROM

Wilkes University

Youngstown State University

The Wean Foundation

North East Ohio MFA program

The Ohio Arts Council

The Stephen & Jeryl Oristaglio Foundation

Nin & James Andrews Foundation

Council of Literary Magazines and Presses

Ruth H. Beecher Foundation

Bates-Manzano Fund

New Mexico Community Foundation

The Raymond John Wean Foundation

NEOMFA
one program : four univers!

Ohio Arts Council
A STATE AGENCY
THAT SUPPORTS PUBLIC
PROGRAMS IN THE ARTS

etruscan press
www.etruscanpress.org

Etruscan Press books may be ordered from

Consortium Book Sales and Distribution
800-283-3572
www.cbsd.com

Small Press Distribution
800-869-7553
www.spdbooks.com

Etruscan Press is a 501(c)(3) nonprofit organization.
Contributions to Etruscan Press are tax deductible
as allowed under applicable law.
For more information, a prospectus,
or to order one of our titles,
contact us at etruscanpress@gmail.com.